What's your favourite kind of flower?

CURIOUS Questions & answers about...

Plants

Have you ever grown a plant from a seed?

Have you ever hugged a tree?

If you could be friends with a bat or a bee, which would you choose?

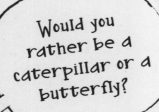

Would you rather be a caterpillar or a butterfly?

What's your favourite fruit or vegetable?

Words by Camilla de la Bédoyère

Illustrations by Tim Budgen

Miles Kelly

What is a plant?

Plants are living things that can...

Leaves

① Make new plants

Plants may not have babies but they can make new plants that look just like them! It's called **reproduction** and most plants do this by making seeds.

Stem

Seed

Seeds grow into new plants, which then make more seeds

② Breathe

Plants **breathe** air through tiny holes in their leaves.

We breathe in carbon dioxide from the air and breathe out oxygen.

③ Get rid of waste

Plants are brilliant because when they breathe they make a **waste** gas called oxygen — it's the gas we need to stay alive!

Thanks for giving me clean air to breathe!

④ Use senses

A plant may not have eyes but it can sense light and it can feel, smell, hear and...

⑤ ...move

Plants **move** their leaves to face the Sun. Seeds **travel** too. Some of them are carried a long way on the wind.

I'm off to find a great place to grow into a new plant!

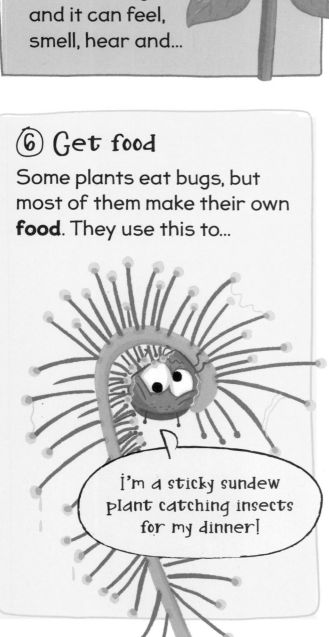

⑥ Get food

Some plants eat bugs, but most of them make their own **food**. They use this to...

I'm a sticky sundew plant catching insects for my dinner!

From little acorns...

...mighty oaks can grow.

⑦ ...grow

Most plants — even giant trees — start their lives as seeds, but they soon grow and change.

Do plants get hungry?

Plants don't feel hungry the same way that animals do, but they do need food. Animals eat their food, but plants make all the food they need.

Sunlight

Flowering plant

Flower

Leaf

Stem

> I can store the food I make in different parts of me and save it for the winter.

Oxygen out

Carbon dioxide in

Why are leaves green?

Because they have a green substance called chlorophyll inside them. This helps the plant collect the energy from sunlight and turn it into food.

> Plants use sunlight to turn water and carbon dioxide from the air into food. This is called photosynthesis.

Water is sucked up from the soil by a plant's roots

Roots also suck up minerals to help a plant grow

How do plants feed the world?

Plants are the beginning of most food chains. This is when living things depend on each other for food. Animals eat plants — fruits, vegetables, nuts and seeds — and some animals also eat other animals.

A food chain shows how energy and nutrients pass from one living thing to another.

I turn the Sun's energy into my food.

I get my energy from eating plants.

Eating small animals and plants gives me the energy to run and play.

Why do plants lose their leaves?

In the autumn many leaves change colour and fall off. This is so the plant can store up water and energy over the winter, ready to grow new leaves in the spring.

Winter

Spring

Autumn

Summer

Did you know?

Plants are cool! When they absorb **sunlight** to make their food they make the air cooler. This helps to control the Earth's temperature.

Solar panels work just like **leaves** because they collect energy from sunlight. We use that energy to make electricity.

Nutrients are the foods, minerals and vitamins we need to live and grow.

Eating **bananas** can make you happy! They contain nutrients that help you to feel good and sleep well.

Mimosa plants are shy! If something touches them they quickly fold up their leaves. It's a clever way to avoid being eaten.

Argh!

Yuk!

When some plants hear the sound of **caterpillars** munching nearby they make nasty tasting chemicals so the caterpillars leave them alone!

The largest leaves belong to **arum plants**. Some have heart-shaped leaves that grow more than 3 metres wide.

Just one **elephant** eats 200 kilograms of plant food every day.

I'm a Japanese morning glory and I change from purple to blue throughout the day.

Some flowers get a suntan! They **change colour** through the day as they warm up.

Mmm, you smell nice. I'm going to wrap myself around you.

Plants don't have noses but some of them can smell. **Dodder plants** grow on other plants. They sniff out their favourites and grow towards them!

Which plants snap, munch and stick?

Some plants don't just make food from sunlight. They eat things too! They are called carnivorous, or meat-eating, plants.

Yum!

We live in dark, boggy places where there's not much sunlight to help make our food, so we eat small creatures to survive.

How do plants catch bugs?

Venus flytraps have trap-shaped leaves coated in hairs. When a spider, beetle or fly crawls over the hairs, the plant's trap snaps shut! The bug tries to escape, but there is no way out.

Snap!

Venus flytrap

Which plants drown their food?

Pitcher plants grow jug-shaped leaves that fill with water. Small creatures are tempted by the plant's smell and fall in, often drowning in the liquid at the bottom of the 'jug'.

Some pitcher plants are big enough to catch frogs and mice!

Stick!

Pitcher Plant

Which plants trap with glue?

Sundew Plant

Once I trap my prey, I make liquid that dissolves the bug into a gloopy soup.

Sundew plants have delicious-looking red droplets that attract passing bugs. They are actually sticky glue, and when a bug lands on them it sticks. The plant then folds over and begins to dissolve the bug. Yum!

Why are flowers pretty?

Flowers have a very important job to do — it's called pollination — and many of them need insects to help. Colours, smells and shapes of flowers attract insects to a plant to pollinate it.

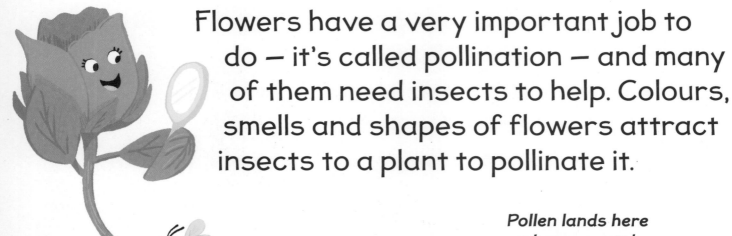

Pollen grows on stamens — the male parts of a flower

Pollen lands here and grows a tube down to the ovary to make new seeds

Colourful petals attract insects

Pollen grains are tiny and look like yellow or orange dust

What is pollination?

Plants make pollen. It comes from the male part of a flower and joins with a flower's egg to make a new plant seed. Insects carry pollen from one flower to another flower's eggs. This is called pollination.

Flowers make nectar at the bottom of petals. It's a sugary liquid that bugs love!

Eggs are inside a flower's ovary. This is the female part of a flower

Why do bees have baskets?

Some bees have special pouches on their legs that they use as baskets to carry the pollen they collect from flowers.

I gather pollen from flowers to use as food in my bee colony.

Bee

Pollen

Banana flower

Bat

Why do bananas need bats?

Banana, cocoa and mango plants are pollinated by bats. They visit the flowers to drink nectar, get covered in pollen and carry it from plant to plant. Birds and moths also pollinate some plants.

I smell sweet at night to tempt moths to come and pollinate me.

Moth

Honeysuckle

How many?

1

The number of days it takes a swarm of locusts to munch through 190,000 tonnes of plants.

The world's tallest flowering plant is a eucalyptus tree called Centurion that grows in Australia. It's **100** metres tall!

2000

The age in years of an ancient seed found by scientists. They planted it and it grew into a healthy magnolia tree!

It takes just **1/50th** of a second for the bladderwort pond plant to catch mosquito larvae in its traps.

I am the fastest killer in the plant kingdom!

150 years old — the age of a giant bromeliad before it grows its first flower. It dies afterwards.

It can take **10** days for a Venus flytrap to digest a dead bug.

A saguaro cactus grows just **4** centimetres in ten years, but bamboo can grow **90** centimetres in a single day!

200

The number of litres of water one corn plant needs to grow. That's more than two full bathtubs!

500 different types of plant are pollinated by bats.

There are **12,500** different types of tree growing in the Amazon rainforest.

Why are tomatoes red?

Tomatoes and other fruits are colourful to tell animals that they are ripe and ready to eat.

I'm tiny and green because I'm not ready to eat!

I'm red, plump, juicy and sweet. Eat me!

Tomato plant

Fruits have seeds in them. When animals eat the fruits, and then do a poo, they spread the seeds to new places where they grow into new plants.

Apple

Seeds

Warning!

Only eat fruits and nuts you have been told are safe to eat.

Why do fruits grow?

When a plant grows some new seeds, the fruit of the plant grows around the seeds to protect them.

Can seeds grow inside me?

Seeds can't grow inside animals or people. They need soil, water and oxygen to start growing.

Water goes into the seed and it swells

There is food in the seed for the new plant

16

Squirrel

Agouti

Why are nuts hard?

Nuts are hard fruits. They are hard to protect the seeds inside, or to help them move safely to new places.

I'm the only animal with teeth strong enough to break open a Brazil nut pod to reach the nuts inside.

I bury acorns so I can eat them in winter. If I forget where I put them they can grow into oak trees!

Have you ever tried to grow a seed? It's easy peasy!

The seedling has a shoot and little leaves

Pea plant

The new plant starts to grow

Roots grow into the soil to collect more water and stop the plant from blowing away

17

Did Diplodocus eat flowers?

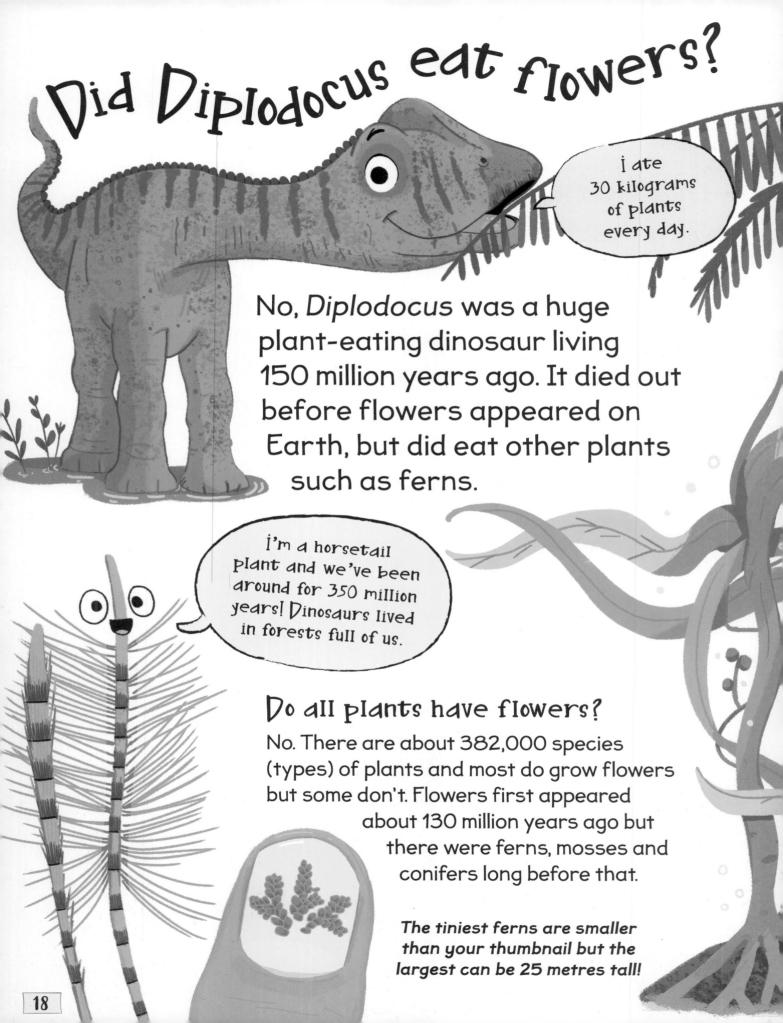

I ate 30 kilograms of plants every day.

No, *Diplodocus* was a huge plant-eating dinosaur living 150 million years ago. It died out before flowers appeared on Earth, but did eat other plants such as ferns.

I'm a horsetail plant and we've been around for 350 million years! Dinosaurs lived in forests full of us.

Do all plants have flowers?

No. There are about 382,000 species (types) of plants and most do grow flowers but some don't. Flowers first appeared about 130 million years ago but there were ferns, mosses and conifers long before that.

The tiniest ferns are smaller than your thumbnail but the largest can be 25 metres tall!

What is an evergreen?

It's a plant that keeps its leaves all year round. Conifers are evergreen trees that are often triangular – the perfect shape for growing in snowy places, as snow slips right off the branches without snapping them!

Conifers grow their seeds inside cones instead of in flowers or fruits

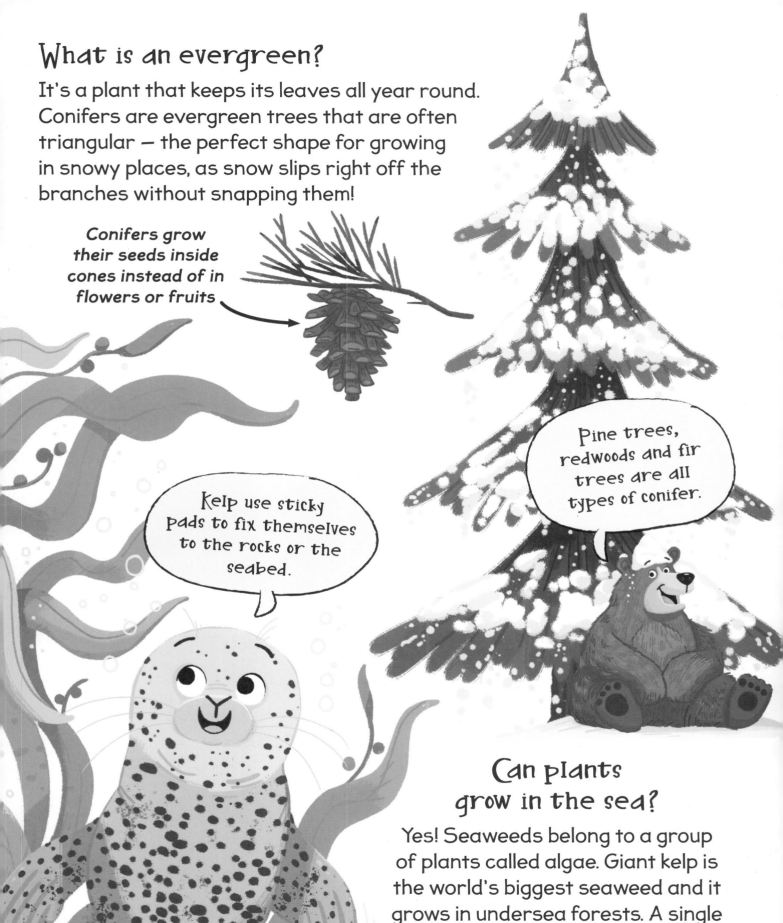

Pine trees, redwoods and fir trees are all types of conifer.

Kelp use sticky pads to fix themselves to the rocks or the seabed.

Can plants grow in the sea?

Yes! Seaweeds belong to a group of plants called algae. Giant kelp is the world's biggest seaweed and it grows in undersea forests. A single strand of kelp can grow to 30 metres long!

How do plants stay safe?

Many animals eat plants, and that's not good news for our green friends! They need to defend themselves from attack and some use prickly thorns and poisons to do this.

Spiky thorns!

Deadly nightshade

Who hugs trees to death?

i do! i'm a strangler fig. i wrap myself around a tall tree to hold me up. Eventually, the tree dies, but i survive!

Warning!

Only eat berries you have been told are safe to eat.

Why are some berries deadly?

Berries often look tasty, but some contain poison to put animals off eating them. Deadly nightshade and foxglove plants can stop your heart from beating, but doctors can also make medicines from them.

Strangler fig

20

Cactus

My fat stem stores water as it rarely rains in a desert. I'm covered in needle-like leaves called spines.

I'm a prickly sweet chestnut. My case only cracks open when the nuts inside are ripe to be eaten by animals who then spread my seeds far and wide.

What's the point of thorns and prickles?

Many plants have sharp thorns and prickles to stop animals from eating them.

Sweet chestnut

We are soft, juicy and tasty, so many animals would like to eat us — but we have a surprise for them!

Nettle

Ouch!

Why do nettles sting?

Nettles have tiny stinging hairs, each with a bead of acid on its tip. If you touch a nettle the hairs prick your skin and the beads release the acid.

Would you rather?

Would you rather sit under a **palm tree** where coconuts might fall on your head, or swim through the roots of a **mangrove tree** where young crocodiles live?

Would you rather be able to make **plants** grow quickly or make it **rain** whenever you want?

It's time to sleep. Would you prefer to lie down in a leaf tent with a **Honduran white bat**...

...or in a grass house with a **harvest mouse**?

Would you rather live to be hundreds of years old like a **cypress tree**...

...or grow to be 9 metres tall like the tallest **sunflower**?

Would you rather munch on **bugs** like a Venus flytrap...

...or be a pitcher plant that eats **frogs**?

Would you rather drink coffee made with **civet poo** or eat durian fruit that smells of **old socks**?

23

Why do giraffes have long tongues?

Giraffes have long, thick tongues that they wrap around a prickly acacia tree to eat its leaves. Acacia trees don't like having their leaves eaten by giraffes, so they also make yummy food for biting ants.

Ouch!

Durian fruits smell like a mixture of dead fish, smelly socks and poo, but I don't mind. I know the flesh inside is delicious!

If a giraffe tries to eat the acacia leaves we can bite its nose!

Yum!

Acacia leaves contain sweet nectar that ants love to eat

Acacia tree

Why is the durian fruit so smelly?

The big, prickly durian fruit stinks so that animals who like it can easily sniff it out and eat it. They then spread its seeds over a wide area in their poo.

Yum!

Sea slug

Sea grapes seaweed

Why do slugs dress up as plants?

This sea slug looks just like its favourite food – sea grapes seaweed! The slug uses this food to turn itself green and even grows lumps on its back for camouflage as it feeds!

Which plants stink of rotting socks?

Lots of plants make foul smells – and some smell like rotting socks! What's more, some animals love this! Arums often smell like rotting meat to attract flies, which buzz among the arums pollinating them.

My flowers grow 3 metres tall to spread my foul smell far and wide.

Yuk!

Titan arum

How big is the tallest tree?

The tallest tree is a coast redwood called Hyperion in California, USA, and it's taller than a 27-storey building! It is about 116 metres tall, and it grows 4 centimetres taller every year. How much have you grown in the past year?

i have more than 550 million leaves!

Coast redwood

Why do people hug trees?

You can hug a tree to work out how big and how old it is. As trees age they get taller but their trunks also get wider. If it takes six children or more to hug an oak tree then it's very old.

Is a mushroom a plant?

No, mushrooms are a type of fungus but, like plants and animals, they are alive. They can grow on dead trees using the wood as their food.

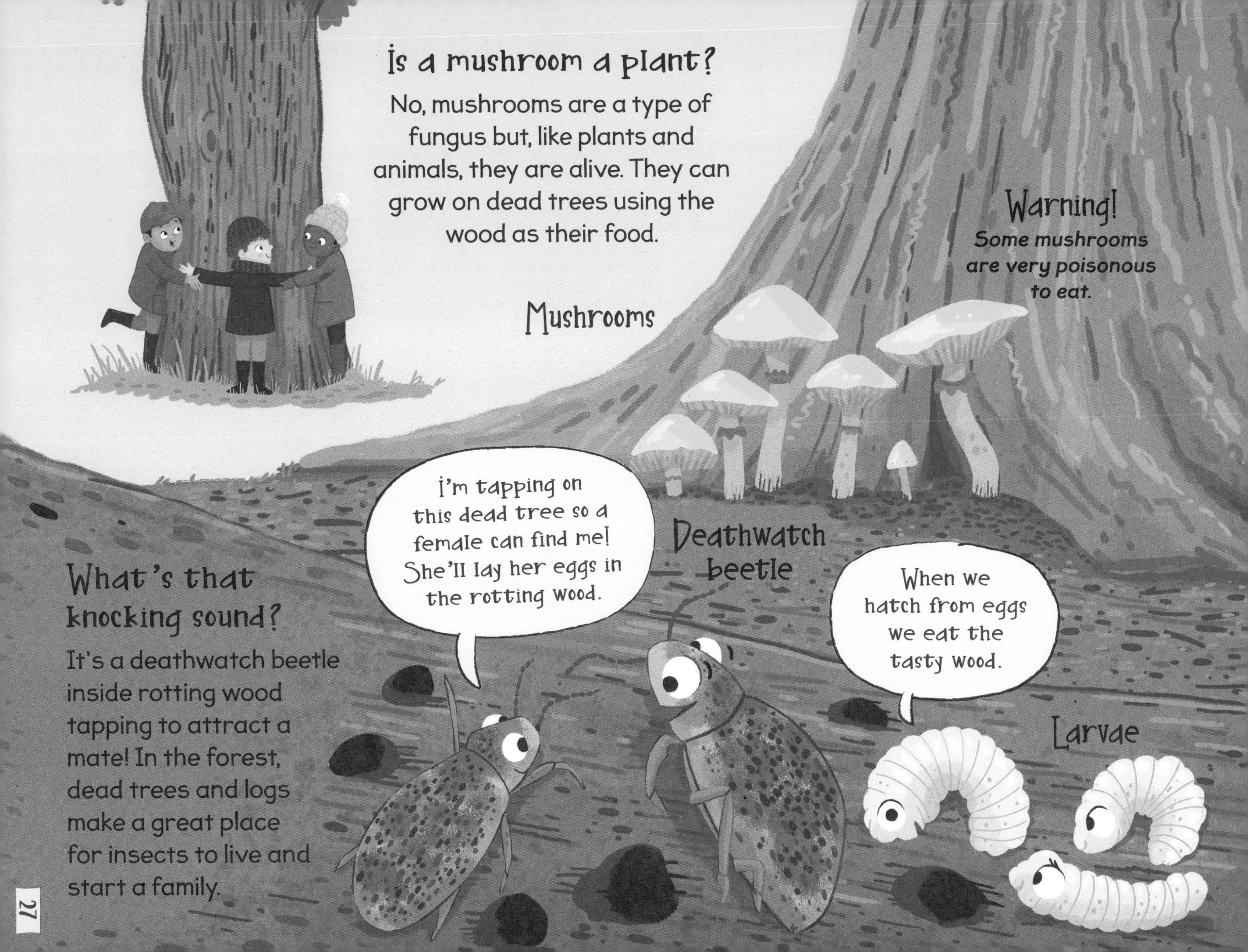

Mushrooms
Warning!
Some mushrooms are very poisonous to eat.
I'm tapping on this dead tree so a female can find me! She'll lay her eggs in the rotting wood.
Deathwatch beetle
When we hatch from eggs we eat the tasty wood.
Larvae

What's that knocking sound?

It's a deathwatch beetle inside rotting wood tapping to attract a mate! In the forest, dead trees and logs make a great place for insects to live and start a family.

Who loves plants?

We do! We eat plants. We also use them for lots of other things...

We use **wood** to make paper and cardboard. This book is made from a **tree**!

Oil is made from lots of different plants — such as sunflowers, olives and soybeans — and used for **cooking**.

Rubber is collected from rubber trees. It's turned into lots of things, such as **toys**, tyres and boots.

We use the **wood** from trees to make **furniture**.

Wood is burned to make fires for **cooking** food and for **heating** homes.

Dead plants can be put onto a **compost** heap. When they rot they put nutrients back into the soil, so more plants can grow.

Plants help to **clean our air** by absorbing carbon dioxide, and they help to keep our planet cool, too. This means they can help us to reduce climate change.

Cotton plants grow fluffy cases around their seeds. These are turned into cotton fabric, which is made into **clothes**.

Scientists use plants to make new **medicines** to help treat diseases.

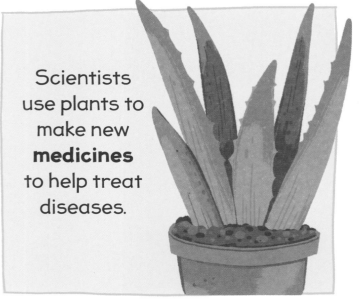

A compendium of questions

How do piranha fish help rainforests grow?

Some piranhas eat fallen fruit from rainforest trees. They poo out the seeds in the river, which then grow into new trees.

Do plants scream?

No, but long ago people believed that a mandrake plant screamed when it was pulled from the ground, and that anyone who heard it would drop dead!

Why do people count tree rings?

A tree grows a new ring every year, so you can count the number of rings on a tree stump to see how old it is.

Can a plant live in space?

Yes. On the International Space Station scientists have grown lettuces, peas and courgettes.

Why do caterpillars eat poisonous leaves?

Monarch caterpillars eat poisonous milkweed plants and store the poisons in their bodies, so birds won't eat them.

Yum!

The Land Called Bulgaria

To PETER

with our thanks and love

John & Tanya.

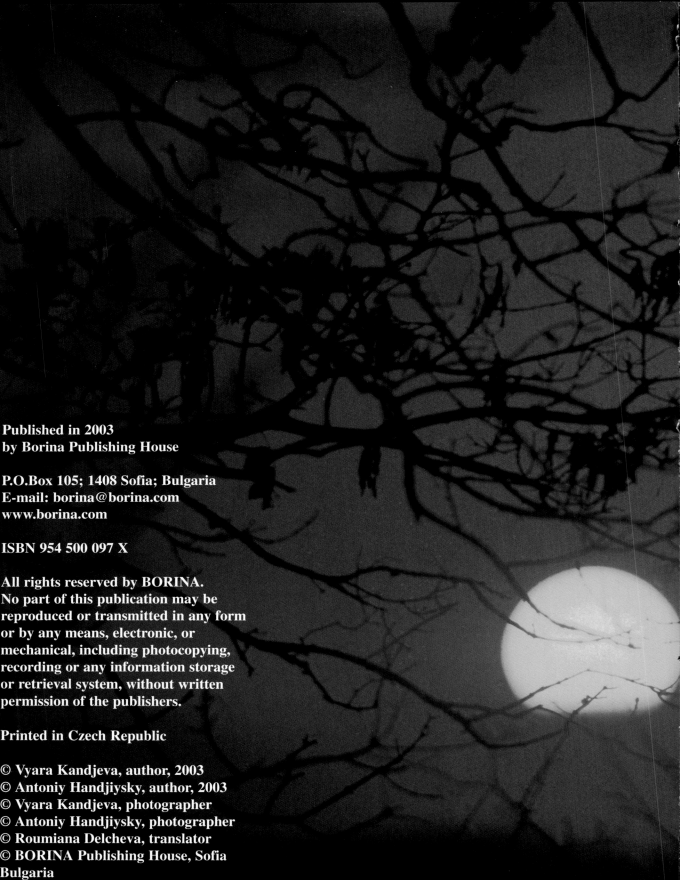

Published in 2003
by Borina Publishing House

P.O.Box 105; 1408 Sofia; Bulgaria
E-mail: borina@borina.com
www.borina.com

ISBN 954 500 097 X

Printed in Czech Republic

The Land Called
BULGARIA

Text and photos
Viara Kandjeva • Antoniy Handjiyski

BORINA

pp. 4-5   One of the Smolyan Lakes, the largest group of landslide lakes in Bulgaria. They cascade over several landslide "steps" at an altitude from 1100 to 1300 m and 6 km away from the town of Smolyan in the Rhodope Mountains. Today it is only seven lakes that are what nature has made on 49.5 ha. The rest have been dried up or converted into fishing farms. The lakes were listed in 1982.

pp. 6-7   Aurochs in the Voden Forest near the town of Zavet, Razgrad district. This animal species, alias the European bison, vanished in Bulgaria in the Middle Ages and was reacclimatized in the 1980s. The aurochs is mentioned in written traditions by the ancient Greek historian Herodotus (484-425 BC) and Pausanius (2nd century); 9th century Old Bulgarian writings describe the aurochs under the name "zomber" and "zubur".

pp. 8-9   The pyramids at the village of Stob, Kyustendil district. They are yellow 3 to 12 m tall Quaternary deposits that rolled down from the Pirin Mountains. Natural sight of international importance.

pp. 10-11   Dandelion (Taraxacum officinale Webber) - a medicinal plant in Lakatnishki Skali locality at the village of Milanovo, Sofia district (Western Balkan

Range). 83.6 ha under protection for the interesting
flora against the backdrop of imposing 320 m high vertical rock faces and 25 caves and karst springs. The
longest cave is 4500 m long.

pp. 12-13 Snezhanka Cave at the town of Peshtera,
Pazardjik district, in the Rhodope Mountains. Space
3200 sq m. Calcite freaks. Cultural remains of the
Thracian tribe Bessi that inhabited that part of the
Rhodopes some 2000 years ago can be seen in one of
the halls. A spiral-shaped bronze fibula (pin), fragments
of hand-made pottery (without using a potter's wheel)
are some of the finds dated to the 6th-4th centuries BC.

A round hearth 4 m in diameter and bones of wild and
domesticated animals that the cave dwellers used in
their diet has survived. The cave and 156.2 ha of land
around the cave became a natural sight in 1961.

pp. 14-15 Floating ice on the Danube, the river that
is the state border between Bulgaria and Romania. It is
relatively seldom to observe an icebound Danube as the
winter is not that bleak every year.

Bulgaria is a lovely nook in Southeast Europe. Wide plains and valleys, high rocky mountains, rounded hills and plateaus, meandering rivers, scenic waterfalls and lakes, hot mineral water springs, lovely shores, deep gorges, canyons and ravines, attractive lagoons and firths and miraculous caves - it is difficult to describe the incredible diversity of landscapes and waterscapes.

The dull language of facts and figures says that Bulgaria is situated in the eastern part of the Balkan Peninsula. Its size is 110,993 square kilometers. The total length of borders is 2245 km of which 1181 km are land borders and 1064 km are water borders (686 km river border and 378 km sea border). The distance between the northernmost and the southernmost point is 330 km; the distance between the westernmost and easternmost point is 520 km.

To the north Bulgaria borders on Romania. 470 km of the border runs along the fairway of the river Danube and 139 km is land border. To the east the country has a coastline of 378 km along the Black Sea; the southern neighbors are Turkey with 133 km of land border and 126 km of river border and Greece with 429 km of land border and 64 km of river border; to the west the country borders on Macedonia (156 km of land border) and Serbia (324 km of land border and 26 km of river border).

The morphology and the long geological evolution of the Balkan Peninsula, which is one of the regions on the Earth with most intense geodynam-ics, have made the Bulgarian relief very varied. The lowlands (altitude up to 200 m) occupy 16% of the country; the plains and hills (altitude 300 m) make up 30% of the territory; the hills and low mountains (altitude 400 m) constitute 25%; the medium-height mountains (altitude from 800 to 1200 m) account for 24% and high mountains for 5% of the territory. In terms of topographic features from north to south Bulgaria is divided into four zones: the Mizian (Moesian) hilly and plateau-type plain (better known as the Danubian Plain), the Balkan Range (Stara Planina), the transitional zone of mountains and valleys and the Macedonian-Rhodope Massif. The 90 to 180 km wide strip along the Black Sea is the fifth morphographic entity called the Western (Roumelian) sector of the Black Sea.

The Mizian Plain constitutes almost one third of Bulgaria (32,000 sq km). To the west it touches the lower reaches of the river Timok and the northern foothills of the Balkan Range; to the north it borders on the river Danube and to the east, on the Black Sea. The predominant altitude is from 100 to 250 m; to the south at the Balkan Range the altitude is from 400 to 600 m; to the north it gradually slopes down and ends with a steep bank at the river Danube at an altitude of 100 to 150 m. At the seaside the altitude descends from 290 m at the Frangensko Plateau in the south to 1-2 m at the village of Durankulak in the north.

The Danubian Plain is scarred by the valleys of scores of rivers most of which are canyons with wide plateaus and flat ridges as watersheds. Often the banks are 100 to 200 m high vertical chalk cliffs with faces punched by gaping mysterious natural and man-made caves. Orlova Chouka (The Eagle's Peak) at the village of Pepelina, Rousse district, is the longest natural cave with underground passages whose total length is 13,437 m. The best-known complex of man-made caves that functioned as churches and monasteries in the Middle Ages is the rock monastery at the village of Ivanovo, Rousse district. The walls and the vaults of the five churches are decorated with murals that are extremely valuable and considered a milestone of 14th century European culture, hence their being recorded on the UNESCO List of World Natural and Cultural Heritage.

The geological processes have produced hundreds of karst springs, lakes, swamps, waterfalls, queer rocks and coral reefs, and lagoons, firths and landslide ponds at the seaside.

Stara Planina is the most prominent range in Bulgaria. Its previous name, Balkan, was adopted for the whole peninsula. The range is 530 km long and occupies 25,500 sq km; it divides the country into Northern and Southern Bulgaria. The range consists of two relatively diverse parts in geologic, tectonic and geomorphologic terms: the northern part is lower and is called the Cis Balkan (Predbalkan) and the southern part is higher and is the Main Balkan Range (Glavna Staroplaninska Veriga). The ridge of the Main Balkan Range is the watershed between the Black Sea and the Aegean Sea with two cleavages formed by the basins of the rivers Iskur and Louda Kamchia - the Iskur Gorge that is 65 km long and up to 500 m deep and the Louda Kamchia Gorge.

From the west to the east the Balkan Range is conventionally divided into a Western, Central and Eastern Part. The Western Part is 45 km wide; the 2168 m high Midjour is the highest mount there. The Central Part is as narrow as 15 km; the 2376 m high Mount Botev is the highest one of the Balkan Range. The Eastern Part gradually expands and ramifies into a Northern and a Southern subpart as it goes to the east. The height descends and at Cape Emine, which juts out into the Black Sea is just 60 m. Bulgarka (1181 m) is the highest mount there.

The transitional zone of mountains and valleys stretches between the Balkan Range to the north and the Macedonian-Rhodope Massif to the south and occupies 30,807 sq km. The relief is very varied: of the 31 mountains Sredna Gora that is 285 km long and with its premier Mount Bogdan (1604 m) is most significant. In addition there are vales between the mountains and extensive plains one of which is the Upper Thracian Plain (Gornotrakiiska Nizina, 6000 sq km and altitude of 165 m on average), the largest plain in Bulgaria and in the Balkan Peninsula.

The Macedonian-Rhodope Massif (Makedono-Rodopski massif) occupies 22,672 sq km of the southernmost parts of Bulgaria and comprises the most extensive and highest mountain lands. The massif consists of the Dardanian Massif (Ossogovo and

Belassitsa) with premier Mount Rouen (2252 m), the Rila-Pirin Group with premier Mount Moussala (2925 m) and the Rhodope Mountains with premier Mount Golyam Perelik (2191 m). The massif includes the most imposing gorges in Bulgaria (Bistritsa and Dospat) that are almost 20 km long and 350 m deep and couloirs (Trigrad and Bouinovo) that are 3 km and 8 km long and 450 m deep.

The Western (Roumelian) sector of the Black Sea consists of the eastern littorals of the Mizian Plain, the Balkan Range, the transitional zone of mountains and valleys and the shelf comprising a strip that is 90 to 180 km wide and 200 km long, ignoring that the coastline is broken. Otherwise, the length of the coastline is almost double - 378 km, which is to be attributed to the cleaving bays at Balchik, Varna and Bourgas and the many capes that jut out into the sea. The section is divided into a Northern, Central and Southern part.

The Northern Part coast gradually rises from 1-2 m in the north to 290 m in the south. The coast is low north of Cape Shabla, with large beaches and firth lakes; many landslides and lakes terrace the high loess shore south of Cape Shabla. The highest shore (290 m) is at the Frangensko Plateau where the largest landslide on the Bulgarian Black Sea is to be found. The Lake Beloslav and the Lake Varna are south of the landslides; one of the largest beach areas is at the mouth of the river Kamchia.

The Central Part comprises the Balkan Range littorals that stretch between the valleys at the mouths of the rivers Kamchia and Aheloi. The shore is high and is not indented, with steep slopes and landslides here and there, capes that gently jut out into the sea, vast beaches at the mouths of rivers. The Sunny Beach (Slunchev Bryag) is the largest and best known.

The Southern Part consists of low shores, which are deeply indented by peninsulas and rocky capes that jut out into the sea and by bays that cleave deep into the mainland. The mouths of rivers are typical firths that are separated from the sea by sand outcrops or small lagoons. There are several big lakes: Pomoriisko, Atanassovsko and Mandrensko. Here and there the abrasion has chiseled picturesque corridors - fjords and small caves - in the volcanic rocks. There are several small islands - Sveti Peter and Sveti Ivan north of the Bay of Sozopol, Sveta Anastasia opposite Cape Choukalya and Cape Atia and Sveti Toma (also known as Zmiiskia Ostrov or the Snake Island) northwest of the mouth of the river Ropotamo.

Climatically, most of Bulgaria is part of the temperate continental zone but for the southern-most areas that are part of the continental Mediterranean sub zone of the subtropical zone and anything typical of the countries of Central and Western Europe is to be observed there: the movement of humid and relatively warm air currents from the Atlantic Ocean and the cold winds from the Arctic Ocean. The Balkan Range is a shield against this cold air and the winter temperatures in Northern Bulgaria are lower than elsewhere in the country. The Mediterranean climatic influence is felt mostly in the basins of the rivers Maritsa, Toundja, Strouma and Mesta that are the funnels letting in the warm and humid air from the Aegean Sea. At the seaside the summer is warm but not hot and the winter is mild. The lowest mean temperatures in Bulgaria of minus 2°C are recorded in January in North Bulgaria, in the vales sandwiched between the Balkan Range and Sredna Gora Mountains and in the high-altitude fields in Southwest Bulgaria. The highest mean temperatures of 32°C are recorded in July and August in the Upper Thracian Plain.

Hydrologically, Bulgaria is not the horn of plenty with 19,761 km of rivers that are 1200 in number. Most of the Bulgarian rivers are short, the water catchment area is small, the flow varies from season to season and many of the rivers run dry in one season or another. It is only 30 rivers that are 100 km and over long and only Maritsa and Strouma have water catchment areas that exceed 10,000 sq km. Iskur is the longest river (368 km) that Bulgaria does not share with another country. In terms of high flow Maritsa is Number One. The rivers of Bulgaria disgorge their waters into the Black Sea or the Aegean Sea. The watershed runs largely along the ridge of the Main Balkan Range: 56% of the country's waters are emptied into the Black Sea and 44% into the Aegean Sea.

There are some 400 lakes and swamps in Bulgaria. However, as they are small and shallow, they have a small hydrological contribution. The 95 sq km of such water bodies contain 287 million cu m of water - 64 million cu m of fresh water in the high altitude and riverside lakes and 223 million cu m of saline water in the seaside lakes. The greatest number of lakes (360) is to be found in the Rila and Pirin Mountains. Most of them are glacial and situated at an altitude from 2000 to 2700 m. Their size is small; their depth varies from 2 to 37.5 m (Lake Okoto in Rila and Lake Popovo in Pirin - 29.5 m). Many of the long Bulgarian rivers - Maritsa, Iskur and Mesta - take their source from these lakes.

A group of scenic karst lakes and swamps are associated with the surface negative bodies. They are small and the amount of water is inconstant. Usually they depend on rain or snow water or on water from karst springs some of which run dry in summer. The greatest number of lakes and swamps (over 20) is to be found on the Devetashko Plateau and on the Belyakovsko Plateau and Strazhevsko Plateau in the Mizian Plain.

Karst springs whose behavior is determined by the climate, strength and the calcinations of the rocks and by the size of the water catchment area are equally interesting. Glava Panega at the village of Zlatna Panega, Lovech district, is Bulgaria's largest karst spring with maximum flow of 6070 liters per second. The water spouts from a large siphon cave whose opening is 7 meter under the level of a deep lake, called Gornoto (the Upper Lake). The size and depth of the siphon have not been measured yet. Divers have penetrated as deep as 31 m under the lake surface but could not trace the faces of the siphon. It is interesting to know that in 1895 the Czech brothers Skorpil advanced the hypothesis that the karst spring receives its water from the river Vit that disappears into the waterbed crevices at the village of Glozhene, Lovech district. In 1955 the hypothesis was experimentally verified.

Bulgaria abounds in spas. The annual amount is 109 million cu m, however, half of it is used. The temperature ranges from 8-12°C to over 100oC. With 103.5°C hot water Sapareva Banya is the hottest spa in Bulgaria.

The Bulgarian flora is represented by 12,000 species of which 4200 are higher plants. Natural vegetation covers over 50% of the land; 250 plants are endemics, i.e. species that occur only in Bulgaria and nowhere else. Forests cover 30% of the land. Predominantly these are deciduous forests of leaf-shedding tree species - oak (Quercus), beech (Fagus sylvatica), hornbeam (Carpinus betulus), maple (Acer campestre), elm (Ulmus), birch (Betula), chestnut (Castanea), ash (Flaxinus), willow (Salix), plane (Platanus); the mountains have a well-grown coniferous belt of spruce (Picea abies), wild pine (Pinus sylvestris), juniper (Juniperus) and the Balkan endemic Macedonian pine (Pinus peuce Griseb.) and Heldreich pine (Pinus heldreichii Christ.). Interesting dense forests of over 40 tree and shrub species can be seen along the rivers in the southern and eastern regions of the country. Evergreen vegetation grows in the southernmost regions.

Geographically Bulgaria is a natural bridge between Europe and Asia. The varied relief and the climate maintain the wildlife. The 35,000 recorded species are believed to be half of what the country actually has. Insects are most numerous (30,000 species); the arachnida place second. 1200 of the animal species in Bulgaria are endemic and occur in a definite area; of them 790 are Bulgarian endemics and 410 are Balkan endemics. The vertebrata are completely studied with 730 species of which 399 bird species and 93 mammal species. This makes Bulgaria one of the countries with the greatest biodiversity in Europe.

A national network of listed natural sights has been institutionalized in Bulgaria. The classification is based on the extent of protection, the mission of the sight and the modus operandi: reserves, national parks, natural sights, maintained reserves, nature parks and protected sites. Silkossia is the first Bulgarian reserve that was established 70 years ago in the Bulgarian part of the Strandja Mountains. It is situated at an altitude of 100-150 m on the left bank of the river Veleka and comprises forests of oriental oak (Quercus hartwissiana Stev.), oriental beech (Fagus orientalis Lipsky), hornbeam (Carpinus betulus), Turkey oak (Quercus cerris), wild service tree (Scorbus torminalis), cheque-tree (Scorbus domestica) and evergreen shrubs of tertiary Crimean-Caucasian endemics species like the Rhododendron (Rhododendron ponticum), medlar (Mespilus germanica) and cherry-laurel (Lauricerasus Roem). The 55 reserves in Bulgaria occupy 76,978 ha.

The Vitosha National Park that was established on October 27, 1934 is the first nature park in Bulgaria and in the Balkan Peninsula and covers most of Mount Vitosha. It is one of the first national parks in Europe after the ones established in Sweden in 1909 and in Spain in 1918. Today there are three national parks in Bulgaria (under high protection) that occupy 193,047.9 ha and 11 nature parks (under lesser protection) that occupy 238,155 ha.

The Pobiti Kamuni (Fossil Forest) at Varna was listed in 1937. The "forest" comprises 300 stone columns between 0.7 and 5.9 m high and from 0.7 to 2.9 m in diameter. Most of the columns stand on their own; they are cylindrical in shape and hollow inside. Other columns are bound together by horizontal slabs of limestone and sandstone. Today the natural sights in Bulgaria are 479 and the total area is 14,548.63 ha.

The 35 maintained reserves on an area of 4451.5 ha are less protected and allow planned intervention for the purposes of science and education and measures that are designed to maintain, control or regenerate.

Areas with typical landscape or habitats of plant or animal species that are endangered, rare or vulnerable are listed correspondingly in order to save the typical landscape components, conserve or regenerate habitat conditions in line with the environmental requirements for the species and populations, facilitate research, education and tourism.

The 142 protected localities in Bulgaria occupy 38,436.49 ha.

With its 565,618 ha of listed areas as of March 31, 2002 that enjoy a various degree of protection and that constitute 5.1% of the country's land and water bodies, Bulgaria ranks third among the European countries (but for Finland and Norway).

Bulgaria is a party to a number of international instruments and agreements of which most important are two conventions and a program with wide-reaching objectives to conserve the global biodiversity - the Convention on Wetlands of International Importance Especially as Waterfowl Habitat (The Ramsar Convention), the World Heritage Convention and the UNESCO Man and Biosphere Program. A total of 22 Bulgarian listed territories on an area of 78,644.6 ha have gained international recognition for the achievements in conservation. In 1993 the Bulgarian Ministry of Environment and Water added another 57 listed sites of international importance - the three national parks, 36 reserves, three maintained reserves, seven natural sights and eight protected localities. Thus Bulgaria has the relatively largest listed territory in Europe with strict vigilance on 79 sites that occupy 430,000 ha, i.e. 86% of all listed territories in the country.

pp. 22-23 *Roussenski Lom Nature Park at the village of Cherven, Rousse district. Situated to the south of the city of Rousse, it includes the lower reaches of the river Roussenski Lom and its tributaries Cherni Lom, Beli Lom and Malki Lom on an area of 3259.8 ha. The picturesque cliffs house dozens of natural and man-made caves. The vegetation is diverse and includes the Mizian Plain's only dense forest. The wildlife is diverse: nesting rare and vanishing bird species like the Egyptian vulture (Neophron percnopterus) and the saker falcon (Falco cherug) that are on the List of Endangered Birds in Europe. There are interesting historic monuments like the Ivanovo rock monastery on the UNESCO List of World Natural and Cultural Heritage.*

pp. 24-25 *Once in the valley of the river Souha Reka, one forgets it is the heart of plain Dobroudja (the Eastern Mizian Plain). The steep and here and there vertical slopes that are as high as 100 to 180 m are on either side. The many canyons in the soft Lower Cretaceous limestone converge into the main valley where crystal-clear rivers used to run on what is now dry parched land. The Souha Reka takes its source east of the village of Izgrev, Varna district. The water catchment area is 2404 sq km. The river is 126 km long before it leaves the Bulgarian territory to flow into the Danube at Lake Oltina in Romania.*

p. 26   *Lake Sreburna, 18 km west of the town of Silistra, on the river Danube (Eastern Mizian Plain). It is the habitat of 160 of the 399 bird species in Bulgaria. Some 90 of them nest and breed in the lake. Sreburna is a maintained reserve on a protected area of 902.1 ha under the Convention on Wetlands of International Importance (The Ramsar Convention), the UNESCO List of World Natural and Cultural Heritage and is a biospheric reserve under the Man and Biosphere Program. This is recognition of the extraordinary contribution to the conservation of the genetic fund of the Earth.*

p. 27   *Pobiti Kamuni (The Fossil Forest) west of the city of Varna. Hundreds of individual columns or groups of columns that are 0.7 to 2.9 m in diameter and 0.7 to 5.9 m tall. Most of the stone columns are cylindrical and hollow inside. Some are bound together by horizontal slabs of limestone and sandstone. The English geologist captain Sprat who visited the Fossil Forest in 1845 was the first one to describe them. The 253.3 ha forest was declared a natural sight in 1937.*

pp. 28-29 Herds of game in the Loudogorie, a plateau in the eastern part of the Mizian Plain with an average altitude of 300 m. Scarred by the canyons of several rivers it still has extensive remains of the onetime oak forests called Wild Woods (Louda Gora or Deliorman).

pp. 30-31 Part of the northern slope of the Central Balkan Range, the narrowest and stoutest section of the Stara Planina. The land north of Mount Baba (altitude 800 to 2000 m) is the Boatin Biospheric Reserve whose mission is to conserve the vastest naturally growing beech forests in the Balkan Peninsula.

pp. 32-33 *Glava Panega karst spring at the village of Zlatna Panega, Lovech district. The water spouts from a siphon cave whose opening is 7 meter under the level of a deep lake, called Gornoto (the Upper Lake). The size and depth of the siphon have not been measured yet. Divers have penetrated as deep as 31 m under the lake surface but could not trace the faces of the siphon. Gornoto (the Upper) and Dolnoto (the Lower) lake that communicate via a subterranean siphon as long as 100 m get their water from there. The river Panega takes its source from Lake Dolnoto. Remains of a Thracian settlement and of a shrine have been discovered around the spring. Listed as a natural sight in 1966.*

p. 34 Lakatnishki Skali - 320 m high rocks towering over the river Iskur. The thick limestone alternates with dolomite, which forms the "feet" while the limestone forms the vertical faces. Of the caves that gape at differing levels Temnata Doupka (the Dark Hollow) is the longest with 4500 m of galleries. Two rivers flow across the cave and 19 lakes stand still inside. Two small rivers - Proboinitsa and Petrenitsa - form scenic canyons in the western part of the locality. The 83.6 ha of the Lakatnishki Skali locality at the village of Milanovo, Sofia district, were listed in 1966.

p. 35 The entrance of the Temnata Doupka (Dark Hollow) Cave.

p. 35 Ritlite - rocks at the village of Lyutibrod, Vratsa district. Height: 60-80 m; length: up to 500 m; area: 123.3 ha. Listed in 1938.

pp. 36-37 *Beech forest in the Etropole section of the Stara Planina, the easternmost part of the Western Balkan Range. Apart from the Strandja Mountains the beech (Fagus sylvatica) grows in all Bulgarian mountains on some 500,000 ha that form a belt at an altitude from 900 to 1500 m.*

37

pp. 38-39 Waterfalls are the most attractive spots in the river basins. They form where the longitudinal profile of the riverbed bends vertically to let the water fall as a foamy pillar. Here and there the bends are several and the water cascades. Of the 300 and more waterfalls of varying height in Bulgaria 71 are listed natural sights.

The waterfall at the village of Hotnitsa, Veliko Turnovo district.

The Momin Skok Waterfall in the Emen Canyon at the village of Emen, Veliko Turnovo district.

The Skaklya Waterfall at the village of Zassele, Sofia district, consisting of a number of cataracts with total height 161 m, the highest of them being 92 m.

The travertine Varovitets Waterfall near the town of Etropole, Sofia district.

Some 23% of the territory of Bulgaria is covered with carbonate rocks. The millennial physical effects and chemical reactions between the water and the rocks have produced diverse carvings on the surface and under it known as karst carvings. Caves, a magnificent world deep into the earth, are the most interesting. 124 of the 4500 caves in Bulgaria are natural sights. Duhlata at the village of Bosnek, Pernik district, is the longest cave in Bulgaria. The mapped passages in this gigantic maze of curving tunnels and halls chiseled by the water of the river Strouma in the bowels of Mount Vitosha have a length of 16,500 m. Listed as a natural sight in 1962.

pp. 40-41 *Calcite forms in the Ledenika Cave near the town of Vratsa. It was listed in 1960, provided with lighting fixtures and safe passages and has been visited by 1.5 million people since then.*
Icicles in the Ledenika Cave near the town of Vratsa.

p. 41 *The Big Stalactite, a calcite freak in the Magoura Cave. 20 m high, 4 m at the base. The Magoura Cave is near the village of Rabisha, Vidin district. Listed as a natural sight in 1960. Provided with lighting fixtures and safe passages. One of the most visited sites in Bulgaria. Archaeological excavations have exposed the foundations of dwellings in one of the halls, plus hearths and tools from the Early Bronze and Early Iron Age. Paintings on one of the walls of the galleries depict hunting and worship scenes that are dated to the Early Bronze Age.*

p. 41 *Bats. They are the only flying mammals that winter in caves in assemblages of 1000 and more bats. The five bat species in Bulgaria enjoy protection under the Nature Protection Act.*

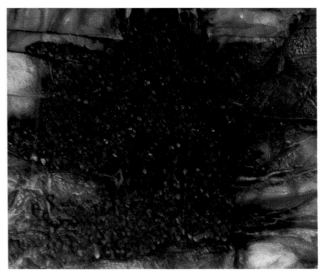

p. 42   *Varovitets, a travertine waterfall at the Varovitets Monastery near Etropole.*

p. 42   *Vranata Voda, a travertine waterfall at the village of Ribaritsa, Lovech district.*

p. 43   *Vratsata, a gorge on the river Leva in the Vratsa section of the Balkan Range, 3 km south of the town of Vratsa. Listed on February 3, 1964 together with 2 ha of adjacent area.*

p. 43   *Bozhiyat Most (God's Bridge) - a rock bridge on the river Lilyachka at the village of Lilyache, Vratsa district. Height of the entrance: 25 m; width: 20 m; length of the arch: 125 m. Of the three lakes along the bridge the largest one is 60 m long and 11 m wide. This working of nature is what has remained from a karst cave most of whose arch tumbled down and cut a deep canyon. The survived parts of the arch are harder limestone. Listed as a natural sight in 1964 together with 12.8 ha of adjacent area.*

p. 43   *The "lunettes" in the vault of the Prohodna Cave at the village of Karloukovo, Lovech district. The cave is 243 m long; the vault is from 25 to 41 m high. It was a dwelling place in the New Stone and Copper Stone Age. Listed as a natural sight in 1963.*

pp. 44-45 *The Belogradchik Rocks, a gigantic petrified world with amazing figures that the elements have chiseled. The rocks are dispersed on a strip of land that is 30 km long and 5 km wide and are conglomerate stone and sandstone, which are reddish because of the iron oxides. Their differing hardness and fusion account for the differing speed of the weathering and erosion processes that have produced this fantastic petrified world. The popular imagination saw in the figures men and animals, invented stories about them and gave them names. Listed as a natural sight in 1949 with a total area of 598.7 ha.*

p. 46   *The   Tzarichina Reserve in the Central Balkan Range, in the common of the village of Ribaritsa, Lovech district. Area: 3418.7 ha. Its mission is to save the only Balkan pine (Pinus peuce) forests in the Balkan Range. It is a Balkan endemic species (i.e. it occurs nowhere but in the Balkan Peninsula). The reserve was established in 1949. Today it is a protected area of international importance in the Man and Biosphere Program.*

p. 47   *Wood ant (Formica rufa), a common species in Bulgaria. The anthills that this ant builds are up to 2 m high and up to 3 m in diameter.*

pp. 48-49   *The Rhodopes, a 14,735 sq km massif in southern Bulgaria. 240 km long and 100 km wide. Golyam Perelik (2191 m) is the highest mount.*

p. 50 *Trigradsko Zhdrelo (Trigrad Gorge). The gorge proper is 2 km long and 300 m deep. It has been chiseled by the river Trigradska which today flows deep under the surface of the earth into the vertical cave Dyavolskoto Gurlo (The Devil's Throat) before it emerges on the surface as a karst spring in the narrowest part of the gorge where the distance between the surrounding rocks is 100 m. Listed as a natural sight of international importance in 1963 with an adjacent area of 296.6 ha.*

p. 51 *Dyavolskoto Gurlo (The Devil's Throat), a vertical cave where the river Trigradska flows over a distance of 700 meters under the surface of the earth. The cave comprises a series of halls the largest of which is 110 m long, 40 m wide and 36 m high. The halls communicate through galleries and waterfalls the deepest of which is 41 m and is the point where the cave starts. Part of the cave has been provided with torchlight and steel passages and stairs, which take visitors to a world of majestic grimness.*

p. 52 The Chairi lakes. A group of landslide lakes in Chairite locality at Trigrad, Smolyan district. Listed with an area of 314 ha.

p. 53 The confluence of the rivers Chairska and Trigradska at the Trigrad Gorge.

p. 53 The river Arda, the longest river in the Rhodope Mountains. It takes its source from Ardabashi, a karst spring at the foot of Mount Ardin Vruh in the Western Rhodopes. The river flows over a distance of 241 km in Bulgaria before it flows into the river Maritsa at Edirne in Turkey.

p. 54-55   Lilium rhodopaeum, a perennial bulbaceous plant that grows in several places of the Rhodope Mountains in Bulgaria and in one place in Northeastern Greece. A Balkan endemic species recorded on the Red Book of Bulgaria and on the List of European Rare, Endangered and Endemic Plants. The 1 ha large habitat at the village of Sivino in Livadite locality was listed as a protected site in 1966.

p. 56   Choudnite Mostove (The Miraculous Bridges), three rock bridges in the vicinity of Mount Golyam Persenk in the Rhodopes near the village of Orehovo, Smolyan district. The bridges are what remained of a large karst cave. The biggest bridge is 95 m long, 48 m wide and 30 m high. Listed in 1949 with the adjacent area of 39.7 ha.

p. 57   Bouinovsko Zhdrelo (Bouinovo Gorge) in the common of the village of Bouinovo, Smolyan district, in the Western Rhodopes. The water of the river Bouinovska has chiseled the 7 km long gorge in the company of cliffs as high as 350 m and a width of 5-6 m where the distance between the cliffs is shortest. The gaping holes of several caves of which Yagodinska is the most interesting tower the river at various heights. The cave is a three-level structure with galleries whose total length is 6500 m. It was a dwelling place in the Eneolithic, Bronze and Iron Age. The cave has been provided with lighting fixtures and safe passages. The Bouinovo Gorge is a listed sight with an adjacent area of 608.6 ha.

p. 58 *Gubite (The Mushrooms) at the village of Beli Plast, Kurdjali district. They are the product of weathering and erosion in the volcanic tuffs. The coloring varies because of the iron, manganese and other oxides. Listed as a natural sight in 1975 with an adjacent area of 3 ha.*

p. 59 *The pyramids at the village of Zimzelen. Dozens of queer pyramids of various nuances owing to the volcanic tuffs on an area of 5 ha. Listed as a natural sight in 1975 with an adjacent area of 5 ha.*

p. 59 *The pyramids at the town of Melnik - majestic gray and white 100 m tall sandstone sculptures. Listed as a natural sight of international importance with its adjacent area of 1156.6 ha.*

pp. 60-61 *The Petrified Wedding - a freak of nature at the village of Zimzelen, Kurdjali district.*

Pirin National Park, Bulgaria's third largest national park in Northern and Central Pirin. Area: 40,332.4 ha. It comprises two reserves on an area of 6029.2 ha. The Bayuvi Doupki-Djindjiritsa Reserve is the venue of the Man and Biosphere international program research. It is on the UNESCO List of World Natural and Cultural Heritage.

p. 62 Pirin National Park - a view of Mount Vihren, the highest peak, 2914 m, in the Alpine belt of the mountains.

p. 63 Pirin Karst - most of the Pirin Mountains is marble which accounts for the bald rocky peaks.

p. 63 Pirin National Park - Lake Ribnoto (the Fish Lake). Area: 6.5 ha; maximum depth: 12 m. It is the largest of the Bunderitsa Lakes group (13 lakes) from where the river Bunderitsa takes its source.

p. 64 Pirin National Park - Lake Okoto (the Eye Lake) in a cirque terrace on the western slope of Mount Todorin Vruh.

p. 64 Popina Luka Waterfall in the Pirin Mountains, on the river Sandanska Bistritsa at the town of Sandanski, Blagoevgrad district.

p. 65 The valley of the river Bunderitsa.

p. 66 *Geyser - a pulsating hot water spring (103.8°C), the hottest spring in Bulgaria and in Europe. It is at the foothills of the Rila Mountains at the town of Sapareva Banya.*

p. 66 *Rila National Park, the largest park in Bulgaria. Area: 81,046 ha. It comprises almost half of the Rila Mountains and includes four reserves of which two are biospheric reserves.*

p. 67 *The Dry Tree - 59 m tall, age 350 years. It is one of the tallest trees in the Parangalitsa Reserve.*

p. 67 *Parangalitsa Reserve in the Rila National Park. Area: 1509 ha; altitude: from 1400 to 2485 m. The reserve comprises the most imposing Bulgarian forests of spruce (Picea abies), silver fir (Abies alba) and Scotch pine (Pinus sylvestris). 75% of the reserve is a spruce forest, which is 200 to 380 years old. Individual trees are as tall as 60 m. Listed as a reserve in 1933. Declared a biospheric reserve in 1977.*

p. 68 Kozhouh - an extinct volcano with solidified lava on the slopes, gaseous bubbles in the bed of the river Strouma that flows via its crater and hot mineral water springing from the bottom. Small caves have been formed in the volcanic rocks on the slopes.

p. 69 White stork (Ciconia ciconia) - a big migrant bird whose spread wings reach 120 cm. Villages in plains and hilly regions are its habitat.

p. 69 Hot mineral spring in a volcano crater: the temperature is 54°C and the mineral content is 2.6 g per liter.

p. 70 A lake at Blagoev-grad, a stopover of the migrant birds using the Via Aristotelis, one of the two routes going via the territory of Bulgaria.

p. 71 Soskovcheto, a forest reserve near the town of Smolyan.

p. 71 A 20-meter high waterfall on the river Kriva in the northwestern part of the town of Smolyan (The Smolyan Waterfall).

pp. 72-73 Globe flower (Trollius europaeus) in Vitosha Nature Park - a perennial herbaceous plant growing on wetland and turf at mountain brooks in the coniferous and the sub-Alpine belt. Protected species in the Red Book of Bulgaria.

pp. 74-75 *It is difficult to determine the date of birth of the interest in the charming and graceful world of flowers. It is beyond doubt, however, that their incredible magnificence and the diversity of their shapes and hues and their scent impact the feelings and thoughts of human beings. Some of these interesting plants that grow in natural habitats are entered in the Red Book of Bulgaria and their habitats are protected sites.*

Lilium jankae - a perennial bulbaceous plant, found in grassy places and rocky meadows at an altitude between 1000 and 2500 m. Balkan endemic species.

Anemone narcissiflora - a perennial herbaceous plant, found in grassy and rocky places at an altitude between 1800 and 2750 m.

Tulipa urumoffii - a perennial bulbaceous plant, found in meadows with dry stony soils at an altitude between 50 and 700 m. Bulgarian endemic plant.

Aquilegia aurea - a perennial herbaceous plant, found in rocky places at an altitude between 1800 and 2500 m. Balkan endemic plant.

Paeonia peregrina Mill. - a widespread perennial herbaceous medicinal plant.

Geranium sylvaticum - a perennial herbaceous medicinal plant, very common in all Bulgarian mountains and with wide application in popular medicine.

pp. 76-77 *Vitosha Nature Park, the oldest park in Bulgaria and in the Balkan Peninsula. It was instituted in 1934 and after several extensions acquired 26,606.6 ha. The park is a mountain massif with steep slopes and extensive plane grounds. Cherni Vruh (2290 m) is the highest peak; 27 peaks rise 1500 m and more. The moraines or well-polished syenite debris carried down and deposited by glaciers are typical of Vitosha. The ridge is one of the wettest places in the country. The park is the habitat of 1500 higher plant species and of almost one third (120) of the bird species in Bulgaria. There are two reserves: Bistrishko Branishte (declared in 1934) and Torfeno Branishte (declared in 1935). The former is included in the Man and Biosphere Program and listed as an area of international importance. During the weekends over 100,000 people daily visit the park.*

p. 78   *Golyamata Gramada (The Big Heap) "stone river" in the Bistrishko Branishte Biospheric Reserve. It is the longest one in the Vitosha Nature Park - 1000 m long and 300 m wide.*

p. 79   *One of Bulgaria's major skiing centers is in the vicinity of Aleko Chalet in the eastern part of Mount Vitosha. Two cabin lifts and four chair lifts and rope tows serve winter sports fans. Aleko Chalet is the point of departure of the European hiking itinerary E-4.*

pp. 80-81   *Lake Mandrensko, a firth in the southeastern part of the Bourgas Valley. It is 11 km long and 1.3 km wide. The deepest bottom is 5 m. The lake is a nesting place of a great number of birds some of which are internationally endangered species. It s a stopover of the migrant birds using the Via Pontica and is a protected area of international importance.*

pp. 82-83 *Ropotamo Reserve - little egret (Egretta garzetta). An area of 1000 ha includes the lower reaches of the river Ropotamo and the Arkoutino marsh lagoon with unique dense forests, marshes and sand dunes. The reserve is a partial wintering place for migrant birds of the northern passages. It is the habitat of rare amphibian, reptile and mammal species that have been entered into the Red Book of Bulgaria.*

pp. 84-85 *Atanassovsko Ezero Reserve. It covers 1050 ha of Lake Atanassovsko, which is the northernmost of the three Bourgas lakes. It is in the vicinity of Bourgas and is one of the lagoon lakes - a shallow bay, which is separated from the sea by a narrow sand outcrop. It is never icebound in winter owing to the high salinity of the water. Atanassovsko Ezero is the largest stopover in Europe for the migrant birds that use the Via Pontica. During the migratory season over 500,000 birds of 33 species make a stop there. The place is on the Convention on Wetlands of International Importance Especially as Waterfowl Habitat (The Ramsar Convention).*

p. 86   Vodna Lilia Reserve, the largest habitat of the sea daffodil (Pancratium maritimum) in Bulgaria. The plant is a perennial bulbaceous and Tertiary relict species that is threatened with extinction and recorded on the Red Book of Bulgaria.

p. 87   Arkoutino, a lagoon-type swamp lake, formerly Arkoutino Reserve on the Convention on Wetlands of International Importance Especially as Waterfowl Habitat (The Ramsar Convention). Today it is part of the Ropotamo Reserve. A quarter of the lake's surface is exposed and the rest has a heavy blanket of aquatic and marshy plants.

p. 92 *Cape Kaliakra that juts more than 2 km out into the sea. Declared a reserve in 1941 together with the expanse of the sea that washes the cape shore.*

pp. 92-93 *The shore of Cape Kaliakra is steep and hard limestone and conglomerates. The iron oxides in the cliff crevices lend the purple hue. Here and there the abrasion has chiseled small niches and caves where the waves break. It is Bulgaria's only nesting place of the European shag (Phalacrocorax aristotelis). The shelf is still the habitat of the Mediterranean monk seal (Monachus monachus) and one of the caves at the seaside is its den.*

94

p. 94 *The Broken Mountain - a freak of nature near the town of Djebel in the Eastern Rhodopes. It is a huge mass of rock and earth that has been carried down and accumulated with significant quantities of perlite deposits on the surface.*

p. 94 *Kastraklii Reserve on the banks of the Malka Reka and in Kobilino Branishte in the common of the village of Borino, Smolyan district. The reserve possesses the best-conserved forest of Austrian pine (Pinus nigra Arnold). The trees are 200 years old and individual trees are 30 m tall.*

p. 95 *Strandja, the largest Bulgarian nature park on 116,136.2 ha, with five reserves, several protected localities and many natural sights.*

p. 95 *Silkossia, the oldest Bulgarian reserve (1933). It is on the left banks of the river Veleka between the villages Bulgari and Kosti. Some 97.9% of the reserve is forests - oak (Quercus) (70%), beech (Fagus sylvatica) and Turkey oak (Quercus cerris). South Euxine and Colchis vegetation grows in the brushwood.*

pp. 96-97 *The mouth of the river Veleka - a protected locality of international importance, north of the village of Sinemorets, Bourgas district. The locality comprises the mouth of the river whose water meets the sand
outcrop and inundates a distance of 50 m. The banks are
overgrown with dense forests.*

pp. 98-99 *Centralen Balkan National Park. It compris-*
es the highest altitude parts of the Balkan Range on an area
of 71,669.5 ha, with nine reserves and four of the five bios-
pheric reserves in the Balkan Range. Part of the European
hiking itinerary E-4 follows the ridge of the mountain.
pp. 100-101 *Vitosha Nature Park - a view of Sofia.*

The Land Called
BULGARIA

Autors: Vyara Kandjeva, Antoniy Handjiysky
Graphic design: Antoniy Handjiysky
Photos: Vyara Kandjeva, Antoniy Handjiysky
English Translation: Roumiana Delcheva

Scanning: BULGED Ltd., Sofia
Preprint and Layout: GED Ltd., Sofia

Borina Publishing House
P.O.Box 54; 1408 Sofia; Bulgaria
E-mail: borina@borina.com
www.borina.com

ISBN 954 500 097 X

Printed in Czech Republic